Love to Nancie —

Ann Stevens & Giles Kelley

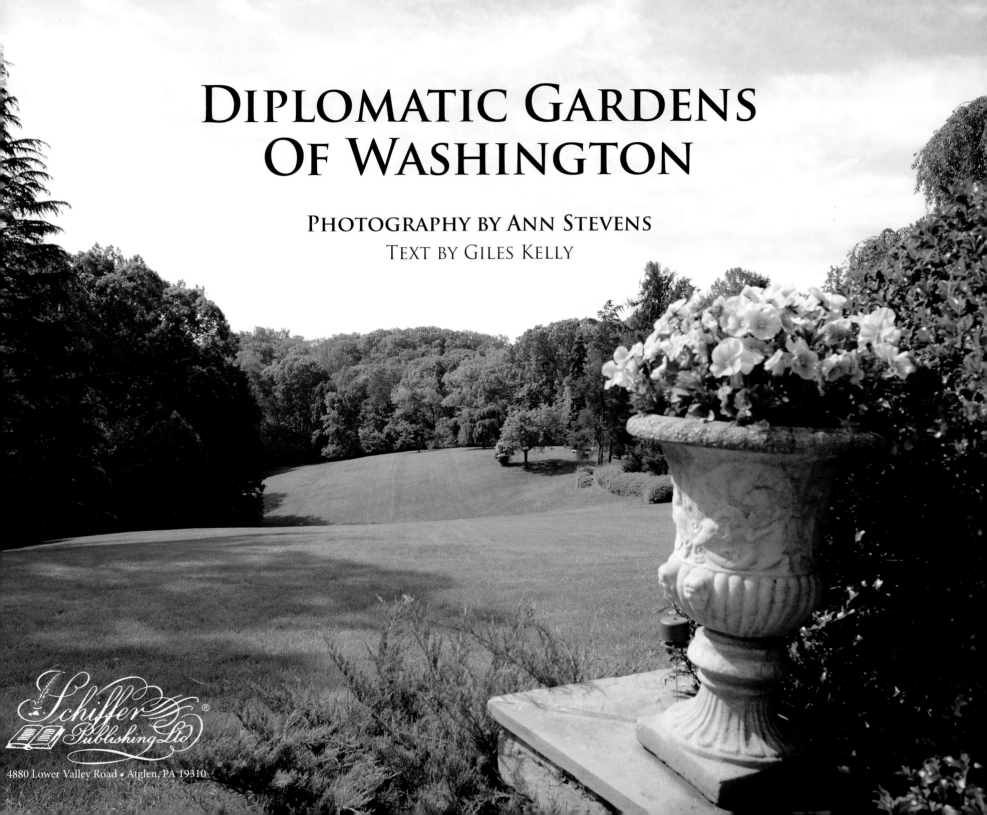

DIPLOMATIC GARDENS OF WASHINGTON

PHOTOGRAPHY BY ANN STEVENS

TEXT BY GILES KELLY

Schiffer Publishing Ltd

4880 Lower Valley Road • Atglen, PA 19310

To Gardeners and Garden Lovers Everywhere

Designed by John P. Cheek
Cover design by Bruce Waters
Type set in Minion Pro

ISBN: 978-0-7643-3978-3
Printed in China

Schiffer Books are available at special discounts for bulk purchases for sales promotions or premiums. Special editions, including personalized covers, corporate imprints, and excerpts can be created in large quantities for special needs. For more information contact the publisher:

Published by Schiffer Publishing Ltd.
4880 Lower Valley Road
Atglen, PA 19310
Phone: (610) 593-1777; Fax: (610) 593-2002
E-mail: Info@schifferbooks.com

For the largest selection of fine reference books on this and related subjects, please visit our website at **www.schifferbooks.com**
We are always looking for people to write books on new and related subjects. If you have an idea for a book, please contact us at proposals@schifferbooks.com

This book may be purchased from the publisher.
Please try your bookstore first.
You may write for a free catalog.

In Europe, Schiffer books are distributed by
Bushwood Books
6 Marksbury Ave.
Kew Gardens
Surrey TW9 4JF England
Phone: 44 (0) 20 8392 8585; Fax: 44 (0) 20 8392 9876
E-mail: info@bushwoodbooks.co.uk
Website: www.bushwoodbooks.co.uk

CONTENTS

EPIGRAPH

"I'd leave all the hurry, the noise and the fray,
For a house full of books and a garden of flowers."

Andrew Lang (1844-1912)
Ballad of True Wisdom

FOREWORD
Why Gardens Matter

believe gardens are essential to our well being because they give us outdoor retreats and places of restoration. They reflect our personalities, our culture, and our needs. Gardens connect us with nature and to the beauty of plants, their forms and textures, and we are thrilled by their colors and their designs.

Gardens awaken our senses through the smells of plants, the sounds of rustling leaves, and by the stunning patterns, shapes, and designs found in plants and trees. Biodiversity brings to our gardens a range of butterflies, birds, and creatures to enhance our outdoor experience, and to better understand the complexities of the natural world.

Can you imagine our world without gardens? How better could we commune with nature? Gardens are a way we interpret nature and redefine it for our own experience.

From the grand designs of gardens at Versailles to the small spaces around our homes, gardens are, or should be, artistic expressions of our world. Depending on our style, they can be totally controlled with clipped hedges and tightly manicured lawns. Or, if our goal is to emulate nature, they can be wild, natural, and loose. Usually they are a combination of both styles with formality and some areas of informality. Most importantly gardens should have a sense of place, of belonging to the site, so that they seem comfortable and right in their location.

Contrasting experiences make gardens exciting. Being in intimate spaces of enclosed gardens, then moving outward to experience grand views, provides contrast as well as surprises. Pathways that create a garden journey take us to different spaces. Places to sit, eat, and entertain provide ways we can live and spend time outdoors. Plants and trees can block out unattractive views, cut down on noise pollution, and grace us with their beauty.

I believe the recognition of the essential nature of gardens is gaining importance on many fronts. With large numbers of people with weight and health problems, gardens are places for physical activity and outdoor living, providing opportunities to get away from computers and televisions. They are a place for connecting with the beauty and power of nature, and for entertaining too.

I find it always refreshing to take a close look at gardens to appreciate their content and unique designs. Washington, DC, has many interesting gardens rich in distinctive features and inspiring qualities.

I think you will particularly enjoy on the following pages visits to 12 of Washington's best kept diplomatic gardens.

Holly H. Shimizu
Executive Director
United States Botanic Garden

PREFACE

We suppose curiosity inspired this book. What is over the diplomatic garden wall? What does the garden look like? How is it used? What is its history?

A recent visit to the Embassy of Denmark during open house on European Unity Day inspired this project. The Danish Ambassador Friis Arne Petersen, upon hearing that we garden, gave us a personal tour of his garden, which he said he liked to tend for pleasure and recreation. We found his garden intimate and informal and wondered about the look of other gardens at ambassadorial residences in the Washington, DC, area and whether they could be photographed.

The capital city of Washington is host to over 170 foreign embassies located for the most part in the northwest section of the city. Some embassies combine the ambassadorial residence with their chancery (office building), and some residences are quite separate and often well away from the chanceries. Those that are separate are likely to be located in the residential sections of the city and marked by a flag or a discrete brass plate on the gate identifying the country of ownership. Otherwise, such residences are hard to distinguish from other homes in the neighborhood.

After researching which ambassadorial residences had gardens or grounds around them, we selected a dozen or so that interested us. With the short list in hand, we wrote directly to each ambassador proposing our idea. We were surprised and pleased by the positive responses. We then arranged to visit each garden.

However, it soon became clear there was a lot more to the project than getting permission to step inside the "garden gate." After we received each ambassador's approval, we were usually referred to a person on the staff to contact. At one place it was the gardener, at another, perhaps, the residence manager or the public affairs officer, and in some cases it was the social secretary. We were also encouraged and helped by several wives of ambassadors. But in every case a schedule for shooting had to be worked out when it was convenient with the household, when the garden was particularly attractive, and when the light was right. The schedules were difficult to make because very seldom did all three of these conditions come together at one time. Working out the shooting schedules over several seasons gave us interesting insights into a dozen foreign cultures and we made some friendships.

We learned that these diplomatic gardens are special. Though they are at private residences they are not owned by the resident. They are owned by a foreign government, and the ambassadors are but trustees for a number of years, for better or worse, after which the responsibility is turned over to the next ambassador. In this sense, these gardens are really quite impersonal. However, much of the current character of a diplomatic garden derives from the legacy handed down by preceding ambassadors and their spouses. And like most gardens, they will forever be "a work in progress."

For their residents, these gardens can provide sanctuary and relaxation. We think the embrace of a garden can take a busy diplomat back to nature for inspiration, reflection, and perhaps a new approach.

Behind these garden walls we discovered some hidden surprises, including a child's playhouse, a lap pool, a telephone booth, a bubbling brook, a sculpture of a reclining horse, a romantic tree swing, a reflecting pool, a statue by a bishop, and one of a friendly bear. We now invite you to turn the pages and find them in the gardens we have portrayed.

Giles Kelly and Ann Stevens

ACKNOWLEDGMENTS

ey to preparing this book was the approval of the following ambassadors who gave us access to their gardens and to whom we owe special thanks: Kim Beazley and Dennis Richardson of **AUSTRALIA;** Sir David Manning and Sir Nigel Sheinwald of **GREAT BRITAIN;** Friis Arne Petersen of **DENMARK;** John Bruton and João Vale De Almeida of the **EUROPEAN UNION;** François Delattre and Pierre Vimont of **FRANCE;** Klaus Scharioth of the **FEDERAL REPUBLIC OF GERMANY;** the late Archbishop Pietro Sambi of the **HOLY SEE;** Giulio Terzi di Sant'Agata of **ITALY;** Han Duk-soo and Lee Tae-sik of **REPUBLIC OF KOREA;** Renée Jones-Bos and Christiaan Mark Johan Kröner of the **NETHERLANDS;** Wegger Chr. Strommen of **NORWAY;** and Jonas Hafström of **SWEDEN.**

We particularly appreciate the guidance and encouragement given to us by the wives of ambassadors from: Australia, Susie Annus; the Republic of Korea, Lee Suk-nam; and Sweden, Eva Hafström.

And thanks, especially, for the patience and generous help the embassy staff members gave us. They personally assisted us with their knowledge and their time. **AUSTRALIA:** Chelsey Martin, first secretary, Public Diplomacy; Susan Richards, Public Affairs; and Andrew Tierney, residence manager. **GREAT BRITAIN:** Lucy Cleaver, personal assistant to the ambassador; John Sonnier, head gardener; and Jim Adams, horticulturist. **DENMARK:** Torsten Stig Jansen, minister counselor, Press, Culture, and Information; Michael Schack Balle Jensen, first secretary, Administration; and Lone Hjortbak

Kanaskie, personal assistant to the ambassador. **EUROPEAN UNION:** Page Napier, social secretary and protocol officer; Maeve O'Beirne, special advisor to Head of the Delegation; and Virgilio Macalinao, residence manager. **FRANCE:** Denise Koptcho, social secretary. **GERMANY:** David Brown, former editor, *The Week in Germany*; Karen Carstens, editor, *The Week in Germany*; and James T. Fowler, Jr., supervisor of Maintenance. **HOLY SEE:** Monsignor John Maksymowicz. **ITALY:** Donatella Verrone, social secretary. **KOREA:** Han Bo-wha, second secretary, Cultural Center; Nam Jin-soo, director of Cultural Center; Adam Wojciechowicz, editor and project manager, Public Affairs; and Yoo Chang-ho, counselor. **NETHERLANDS:** Carla Bundy, press officer; Pauline Roukens, facility manager; and Peter Zalk, gardener. **NORWAY:** Pia Ulrikke Dahl, cultural and information officer; Elin Kylväg, personal assistant to the ambassador; and Anders Skandsen, facility manager. **SWEDEN:** Pia Anderson, social secretary.

Our appreciation also extends to the horticultural advisors, who kindly shared their expertise and time to identify important trees and plants: Chris Andreichuk, gardener; Bill Johnson, horticulturist; Jeffery Lee, landscape architect; Philip McClain, garden designer; and Gordeon Riggle, landscape architect.

Most of all, a very special thank you to my husband Giles Kelly for having the idea for this book and for the unwavering support he gave me during the book's creation. This book is as much his as mine.

Ann Stevens

THE AMBASSADOR'S GARDEN
Embassy of Australia

The bronze plate states that the tree is an American elm and scion of the John Quincy Adams elm planted on the White House lawn in 1826.

Early morning shadows on the front of the residence are cast by the few remaining old oak trees. New saucer magnolias (*Magnolia x soulangeana*) are at either side of the portico, and Green Velvet boxwoods (*Buxus* x 'Green Velvet') along the front, are part of the design for renewing the garden.

The Australian flag flies over the lawn in front of the residence.

This curving border at the left side of the lawn is planted with iris, rhododendrons, perennial geraniums, lilies, and decorative trees.

The Australian Embassy's residence is a spacious and gracious mansion on one of Washington's finest northwest residential streets, Cleveland Avenue. The estate is marked by a polished brass plate at the entrance gate that announces "Residence of the Australian Ambassador."

This fine property was purchased by Australia in 1941 from a Mrs. D. J. Dunnigan, whose late husband had bought the four acres in 1926 and had expanded the original house by the addition of wings that turned it into a 40-room mansion. The architecture is based on the design principles of American homes of the Colonial period. Originally the property was known as "White Oaks" because of a stand of some 20 grand oak trees on the property, of which only a relatively few remain.

Historically, there are two special features to this property. What is now the front of the house was originally the back of the house, and what is now a broad front lawn was once a small forest of oaks in the back. The original front door was reached by a long flight of steps from the street below, which must have been a bit awkward. The present driveway leads very conveniently to the new front entrance, while the former front entrance area is now a terrace and swimming pool.

The other historic feature is that this house was occupied for four years, 1928 through 1932, by a tenant by the name of Major George S. Patton, Jr., U.S. Army, who later was known as General George S. Patton of World War II fame. At that time, Patton was a calvary training officer who enjoyed playing polo, and he stabled a couple of horses on the property.

When Australia first acquired this property it was used for both the ambassador's residence and the chancery. However, in 1951 when a new Australian embassy was completed downtown on Massachusetts Avenue near Scott Circle, the mansion became exclusively the ambassador's residence.

Beyond the entrance gate is a fine brick driveway edged with low walls that curve upward alongside a wide lawn. On the right of this inclined driveway is a

The front portico of the residence viewed from the driveway over the tops of Incrediball™ hydrangeas.

The front lawn, planted with a commemorative American Elm (*Ulmus americana*) at the right, is bordered by a hedge of Green Mountain boxwoods (*Buxus sempervirens 'Green Mountain'*).

Varieties of hydrangeas bordering the curving brick driveway include the hardy white Incrediball™ hydrangea (*Hydrangea arborescens* 'Abetwo') with 12-inch flowers, and the Endless Summer™ Blushing Bride hydrangea (*Hydrangea macrophylla* 'Blushing Bride') with 9-inch flowers that age to a pink blush or light blue depending on the pH level.

The brick driveway curves towards the residence between a pair of stone pots holding rhododendrons.

row of mature holly trees. On the left is a wide bed of roses, azaleas, hydrangeas, and small perennials bordered by a hedge of boxwoods. The driveway then loops around a grassy oval at the front entrance to the residence. Three towering oaks provide summer shade over the oval. A flagstaff on the lawn displays the Australian colors. The lawn is also host to a young tree planted by President George W. Bush with a bronze plate that states the tree is an American elm (*Ulmus americana*) and scion of the John Quincy Adams elm planted on the White House lawn in 1826.

At the side of the lawn is a commemorative Southern magnolia tree (*Magnolia grandiflora*) with a plaque that reads: "Seedling of the Andrew Jackson Magnolias Planted at the White House between 1829 and 1837. Planted by Mrs. Laura Bush, wife of the President of the United States, and Mrs Janette Howard, wife of the Prime Minister of Australia, to symbolize the enduring friendship between the American and Australian peoples. 14 May 2006."

On the right side of the mansion is a three-car garage, next to which is a brick wall with steps that descend to a fenced-in grass tennis court, said to be the only grass court in Washington. Copious clusters of climbing roses in shades of pink and white decorate the far corners of the tennis fence. Attached to the left side of the garage is a modest greenhouse for wintering over tender plants and small lime trees. It looks out over the terrace and swimming pool. From the pool area, the bell tower of the nearby National Cathedral is visible just above the tree line.

At the front of the residence on the left is a row of Mary Nell hollies with a doorway that opens to a small patio just outside the kitchen door. Here, in raised boxes, lettuce, chive, mint, rosemary, and scallions seem to thrive.

The continuing loss of many of the great old oak trees and the aging of much of the residence garden called for major changes to the garden in 2010. A new garden design was initiated that year to provide a better structure to the garden in the absence of the many oaks and with a fear that the remaining ones could also be gone in the next couple of years.

Landscape architects Gordon Riggle and Lila Fendrick created a design to simplify the landscape and provided new sight lines. Their design included additions to the beds along the driveway by adding white-flowering shrubs including azaleas, Incrediball™ and Blushing Bride hydrangeas, and Iceberg and Knockout roses with a curving hedge of Green Mountain boxwoods. The azaleas that existed in those beds were moved to the bank along the front perimeter of the lawn to provide better ground cover and color.

At the front of the residence deciduous saucer magnolias were added at either side of the portico to provide volume. A low border of Green Velvet boxwoods was planted to introduce a sense of depth. Other work still to be done at the front and back of the garden was expected to be finished by the end of 2011. It included creating a better screen for privacy along the front property line with the planting of cherry and evergreen trees, and making a more formalized garden in the back area around the pool and terrace.

Although there is not a cutting garden *per se* at the Australian residence, the borders of the front lawn are well planted with beds of tulips, iris, peonies, and flowering shrubs including spirea and weigela. The setting of this residence, with its long front lawn, its remaining grand oaks, and the fine brickwork, projects a gracious and comfortable look well suited for the residence of the ambassador of Australia, a country that has long been our friend and ally.

A border of rosemary plants grows alongside one of the rectangular planting boxes used for a kitchen garden.

The arched windows on the facade of the house are decorated with a new saucer magnolia at left and tree roses and peonies by the Green Velvet boxwoods.

Climbing roses are espaliered on the inside and outside corners of the walls surrounding the grass tennis court.

Climbing roses by the tennis court.

Lilies, ferns, and a spirea shrub border part of the lower end of the lawn.

Saucer magnolias in full spring glory on the back terrace, visually supported by shaped, golden evergreen euonymus (*Euonymus japonicus*) shrubs.

Saucer magnolia blossoms with euonymus shrubs.

A cascade of spring blossoms on a deciduous weigela (*Caprifoliaceae*), one of the older shrubs in the garden.

THE AMBASSADOR'S GARDEN
British Embassy

The garden was designed by Sir Edwin Lutyens, considered the greatest British architect of the 20th century.

The south facade of the British residence in fall.

This rose garden in front of the residence has climbing roses, hybrid tea roses, and grandiflora roses, including the popular grandiflora rose Queen Elizabeth and the hybrid tea rose McCartney.

A mong the diplomatic gardens of Washington, the one that embraces the residence of the British ambassador stands out for its beauty and unique architecture.

When the British Embassy was completed in 1930, it was the first of several embassies built on the north side of Rock Creek Park. It was completed well before the Massachusetts Avenue bridge was built in 1939, which extended Embassy Row into the suburbs.

Today, the residence, the old chancery, and the new chancery of the British embassy together occupy eight acres on gently sloping land. This enclave is marked by a larger-than-life bronze statue of Sir Winston Churchill created in 1966 by the American sculptor William McVey. The statue stands in a landscaped spot by the public walk along Massachusetts Avenue, placed half on city property and half on British property, symbolizing Churchill's Anglo-American heritage. Until 1985, flowers or greens were placed in Churchill's hand by an unknown admirer throughout the year. Behind the statue, the Union Jack of the British Embassy can be seen just above the tree line.

The residence, the original chancery, and the garden layout, together on four acres, were designed by Sir Edwin Lutyens, considered to be the greatest British architect of the 20th century. The residence is difficult to see from the street because Lutyens placed it behind his U-shaped chancery to provide for more privacy. His design has been described as an English country house in the Queen Ann style. Lutyens specified that the buildings were to be faced with small, hand-made red bricks to create a Tudor look and trimmed with Indiana limestone. The construction began in 1928 at the time of the Great Depression and took two years to complete. It is now one of the largest British embassies in the world.

The garden features some of Lutyens's hallmark designs of arched gateways, brick walls, semi-circular steps, raised terraces, and stone walkways,

A tree rose with Supertunia® petunias on the terrace by the rose garden.

The outside of the garden wall and entrance gates designed by architect Sir Edwin Lutyens.

Climbing roses on the east wall of the main entrance gate of the garden.

characteristics that made him renowned for his landscape designs as well as for his architecture. Lutyens had a long time collaboration with the noted English garden designer Gertrude Jekyll.

When the new embassy residence was ready for occupancy in 1930, the planting of the garden was supervised by Lady Elizabeth Lindsay, nee Hoyt, the American wife of Ambassador Sir Ronald Lindsay. She was a professional landscape architect, having studied at Harvard and Columbia Universities. She worked with Beatrice Farrand, a prominent landscape architect who designed the famous gardens of nearby Dumbarton Oaks estate.

The south-facing residence overlooks a broad spread of lawn with a gentle downward slope. A wide porch, under a portico supported by four stately columns, extends from the front of the residence. When the porch is set with white wicker furniture, it is an inviting place to view the garden.

The perimeter of the lawn is well defined by stands of mature trees and a variety of shrubs that provide the desired privacy. Trees on the grounds of the residence include a Blue Atlas cedar (*Cedrus atlantica*), several beeches, a Regal Prince oak (*Quercus x warei* 'Long'), Japanese and American maples, and Ginkgos (*Ginkgo biloba*). Flowering trees that grace the grounds include dogwoods, magnolias, crab apples, several Kwanzan Cherry trees (*Prunus serrulata* 'Kwanzan'), and a Weeping Higan Cherry tree (*Prunus subhirtella* 'Pendula'). Among the trees on the lawn are several specimens planted by members of the Royal Family.

From the wide porch of the residence, steps descend first to a terrace decorated with black slate as used in Asian gardens thousands of years ago, then to the large lawn, the site for special events. Varieties of hybrid tea roses flourish in beds on each side of the terrace in the formal rose garden, which has about 400 rosebushes producing lovely displays of color from May into late fall. Also the brick walls of the residence host gracefully climbing roses.

Climbing roses in early May on the south wall of the residence.

Varieties of iris flourish in the perennial garden, bordered by Hicksii yews (*Taxus* x *media* 'Hicksii') under the old Kwanzan cherry trees (*Prunus serrulata* 'Kwanzan'), with filtered morning light and afternoon sun.

Clockwise from top left:
Bee Balm (*Monardia*), one of the easiest perennials to grow and a favorite with bees, grows here alongside a white delphinium (*Ranunculaceae*).

The spiky bi-color flowers of Bear's Breeches (*Acanathus* 'hungaricus') make a showy display in the summer perennial border.

Gooseneck Loosestrife (*Lysimachia clethroides*) grows in a showy mass in the summer perennial border. In fall its leaves turn a rich gold.

Peonies (*Paeonia*) bring vivid color in late spring to the perennial garden.

Against the backdrop of the old chancery, the greenhouses are nestled in a side area of the garden. A Blue Atlas cedar, center, provides some varied light conditions for growing plants alongside the greenhouses. In the foreground are River Birch trees, left, and branches of a flowering Weeping Higan Cherry, right.

Beyond the rose beds, walkways lead to inviting destinations such as a small pond, the tennis court, a swimming pool, a small Japanese garden, and an herb garden conveniently located just outside the kitchen door and sheltered from northerly winds by a high brick wall. This small garden was added to the Lutyens design in the 1980s by the then resident ambassador, who also redesigned the herbaceous borders with perennials and low growing plants of greens and grays to give it a more English look.

Over the herbaceous garden wall the sounds of tennis might be heard. The ambassador's court located there is part of the original landscape plan. It is not a Wimbledon-type grass court, but a hard-surface court best suited to Washington's weather. From the court, a short path leads to the swimming pool, which is tucked away in a sunny quarter of the west side of the garden and enclosed by a protective wall. The entrance arch to the pool area is entwined with wisteria. In spring the scent of blossoms fills the air and in summer hanging plants and thriving tropicals provide for a refreshing change of scene.

The perennial garden, in part shade and full sun, borders a stretch of walkway that runs along the western side of the residence. It is planted with such classics as peonies, asters, ladies mantle, iris, delphiniums, geraniums, and dusty millers and benefits from some shade of mature cherry trees. Here also is a line of upright Hicksii yews (*Taxus x media* 'Hicksii') that form a tidy hedge. Another walkway that leads to a small koi pond, shaded by maples, is bordered with shade-loving plants including hostas and astilbes, plus skimmia and Dauphne odora evergreen shrubs, and Oakleaf hydrangeas.

Across the lawn, standing alone under a magnolia tree by the garden wall, is a red British call box, a charming reminder of London to brighten the local landscape. Nearby are two greenhouses in use all year round; in spring to raise bedding plants and in winter to shelter container plants and tropicals to be set in the garden and on terraces in the spring. The greenhouses also shelter a large collection of select orchids, including several historic plants that date back to World Wars I and II. The greenhouses and the cutting garden alongside them provide plants and flowers for embassy functions.

Bedding plants and hanging baskets of petunias in the greenhouse ready for the summer garden.

The pool area is enhanced with potted tropical plants that provide texture and color.

This low-branching Japanese maple lights up an end of the rose garden.

About a dozen local volunteers help keep this residence garden flourishing, and by working with the staff they have a chance to ask questions and learn by doing. Leaves, weeds, and debris are composted, and the organic materials are returned to the garden. No harmful pesticides and herbicides are used. The goal at the British ambassador's residence is to keep the garden completely organic.

This garden seems to embody the spirit of English gardens. It suggests both the informality of an English cottage garden and the formality of an English estate, but with some necessary adjustments for the Washington climate. In any case, this fine garden reflects the importance our British friends place on nature in general and on gardens in particular. And it certainly provides a splendid place for recreation and diplomatic entertaining.

The fall leaves from the towering tulip poplar and the red maples make a colorful setting for a sculpture of a sleeping horse.

THE AMBASSADOR'S GARDEN
Embassy of Denmark

*The garden is meant to promote the
Danish art of "hygge."*

At the front of the residence is this triangular pool with a sculpture of a
goose with the ugly duckling of Hans Christian Anderson's famous story.
The plantings are roses and sedge grass under Bradford pear trees.

The Royal Danish Embassy might seem hidden away. The entrance is found at the end of a quiet street named Whitehaven that branches off from Massachusetts Avenue close to where that avenue crosses Rock Creek Park. Whitehaven is part of the fashionable section of Massachusetts Avenue known as Embassy Row.

A remote-controlled gate slowly opens to an inclined driveway framed with nandinas, hydrangeas, and decorative grasses. The driveway leads to a tidy parking area, well shaded by rows of Bradford pear trees. The modest appearing embassy faces the parking area and consists of two flat-roof buildings which are the chancery and the residence. They are joined by a glass corridor that gives the buildings its Scandinavian look by employing much glass and little decoration except for the bright royal coat of arms of Denmark discretely centered over the entrance to the chancery.

This modern complex was designed by the Danish architect Vilhelm Lauritzen, who said he loved this site for building the embassy because of its abundance of light and greenery, and its proximity to parkland. When completed in 1960 it was Washington's first modern embassy building, and Denmark's King Frederik IX and Queen Ingrid came to Washington to open it.

In summer, the fronts of the residence and chancery are decorated with planters filled with roses, colorful annuals such as cosmos, zinnias, impatiens, and petunias. An interesting feature of the park-like parking area is a small triangular pool in a grove of trees just in front of the residence. Standing within the pool is a column topped with a decorative white swan in flight guarding the little "Ugly Duckling," below, of Hans Christian Anderson's delightful story. This unusually shaped pool, finished in black tile, is surrounded by a border of red roses and other colorful plants. The dedication plaque states this sculpture was donated to the Royal Danish Embassy by Marshall M. Fredericks, its sculptor, on April 20, 1994.

The garden lies behind these two buildings and is best seen from the terrace balcony at the back of the residence. This Danish garden has both a classic and a rustic look. The classic look is the well laid-out rose garden enclosed by a low wall. Inside are four rose beds squared off by narrow grassy paths suggesting the cross shape seen in the Danish flag. A bird bath serves as its centerpiece. As for the more rustic aspect, in one corner of the lawn at the edge of the surrounding forest is a wooden child's playhouse, built by no less than the resident ambassador himself for his young daughter, with staff help.

The garden enjoys a southern exposure with patches of shade provided by stands of tall oaks and pines of the adjoining Dumbarton Oaks parkland. This is a cozy garden that includes large displays of azaleas, blue and white hydrangeas, ornamental grasses, roses, and lavender. As the garden extends all along the back of the residence and chancery buildings, it is intended, in true Danish democratic fashion, for the enjoyment of both the ambassador and his staff without infringement upon each other. At the chancery end of the garden area is a fine swimming pool and patio. Behind the residence, the balcony ends at a stunning wall decorated by the late Danish artist Henrik Starcke with his colorful ceramic tiles portraying birds indigenous to Denmark.

This modest garden reflects an important Danish cultural idea and style. That is to say, it is meant to promote the important Danish art of "hygge." (It is pronounced phonetically something like "Hooga.") It is the word for the uniquely Danish concept of creating an atmosphere of coziness and fellowship. Americans might take "hygge" to mean "laid back," but it is more than that. In Danish, the word also implies a warm place for taking time out with family and friends to enjoy each other's company.

Indeed, this small embassy garden, though far from Denmark, does seem able to provide for "hygge," which can prove very useful in the practice of diplomacy.

In front of the residence in summer, planters are filled with petunias and cosmos with lavender colored Russian sage (*Perovskia atriplicifolia*) at the side.

Pots of dwarf Alberta spruce and colorful annuals decorate the terrace.

Ceramic tile mosaics of Denmark's native birds, by Henrik Starcke, are the focal point at the end of the residence's long terrace. In the pot is a dwarf Alberta spruce (*Picea glauca* 'conica').

The grass strips crossing the rose garden suggest the cross seen in the Danish flag. The garden includes hybrid tea roses, lavender, and purple flowering butterfly bushes (*Buddleia davidii*).

This child's playhouse, built by the ambassador for his daughter, includes the Danish flag, a mailbox, windows, window boxes, a Dutch door, and two porches.

These vivid blue hydrangeas are among several varieties of blue and white hydrangeas grown in the garden.

These overlapping low stone walls provide a walk-through place in the middle of the garden opposite where the residence and chancery buildings are connected.

A terrace for dining is next to the pool at the staff end of the garden.

The ambassador's garden in spring with flowering azaleas and pink dogwoods.

THE AMBASSADOR'S GARDEN
Delegation of the European Union

Four lovely statues of females appear to watch over the garden from the terrace.

The Italianate-style residence of the ambassador of the European Union, with an elegant double-stair entry, is surrounded with flowering and hardwood trees.

This view of the garden from the upper terrace includes the circular terrace, a lovely mature crape myrtle, and the hedge of boxwoods.

The residence of the ambassador of the European Union is a charming Classical Revival-style villa located in a residential neighborhood a few blocks from Massachusetts Avenue, NW, in a section known as Sheridan-Kalorama. When this fine house was built on Belmont Road in 1922, it was the only house on the street. It remained alone there until the late 1940s when a fashionable neighborhood began to grow up around it. Today it is renowned for its fine architecture.

The residence was designed by the nationally recognized architect William Lawrence Bottomley, who had studied at the French *Académie des Beaux-Arts* and at the American Academy in Rome. He drew inspiration for this design from classical ideals and, especially, from the Italian Renaissance. The house was built at a time when various Classical Revival styles were very popular in the United States.

From 1957 to 1969, this house was home to Douglas Dillon who was Under Secretary of State for President Eisenhower and, later, Secretary of the Treasury under President Kennedy. The then Commission of the European Communities, now the European Union, acquired it in 1970.

The Washington landscape architectural firm Innocente and Webel was engaged at that time to renovate the garden and to augment the Italianate feeling by adding a paved patio and a fountain immediately behind the house with a small, very private formal garden. Boxwoods and classic planters for seasonal flowers were positioned around the ornate fountain. A lavender flowering crape myrtle was planted to provide summer shade on the patio. Azalea bushes were placed around the perimeter to soften the garden corners and provide color in the spring.

Beyond the patio, a few steps lead up to a narrow terrace across the back of the garden. Tall arches in the wall along this terrace form niches occupied by four lovely statues of females representing the four seasons of the year. They appear to watch over the garden below. Along the rear wall of the residence, above the entry, espaliered sweet smelling purple wisteria blossoms put on a splendid spring show.

The whole garden is entirely enclosed by the surrounding walls and buildings. One thing that makes this scene particularly memorable is that the house and walls are painted in a terra cotta color with white trim, adding to the Italianate look. During renovations to the residence in 1998, additions were made, including an enclosed garden-room that opens to the pool.

The blue flag of the European Union flies from a tall staff that stands on the narrow front lawn bordered with crape myrtles and azaleas. Europe Day in May is annually celebrated at this residence with a reception on the terrace for several hundred friends of the European Union. At such times, weather permitting, the garden serves as a natural extension of the indoor entertainment spaces, giving the ambassador the added pleasure of hosting his guests in the garden.

Peonies and iris grow in beds alongside the wall of the residence.

The garden design includes several brick walkways that connect at each end of the residence. Pink flowering hydrangeas, just starting to bloom, are interspersed with boxwoods.

Wisteria *(Wisteria)* vines above the arches at the back of the residence add charm to the circular terrace.

This pot of summer flowers is by the shallow steps leading to the pool area. The rounded boxwoods throughout the garden provide volume and structure to the garden spaces.

Potted summer flowers like these add color to the pool area.

The pool lies close to the residence and alongside the garden.

The fountain on the edge of the terrace is enhanced with nandina and pots of geraniums. A hedge of boxwoods partially hides the wall of niches at the back of the garden.

Four statues, "The Four Seasons," are in niches of the garden's back wall. A terrace area with garden chairs is at the far end.

One of four Italianate statues in niches in the upper garden wall.

THE AMBASSADOR'S GARDEN
Embassy of France

*It is easy to envision this secluded garden
filled with guests enjoying champagne and*
hors d'oeuvres.

The Tudor-Jacobean style residence of the French ambassador is framed
by two large magnolia *(Magnolia grandifolia)* trees at either end.

This well shaped Norway maple (*Acer platanoides*) is the focal point in the sweeping lawn to the side of the residence.

Today the French ambassador's residence is a magnificent English Tudor-style mansion located in one of Washington's most fashionable neighborhoods, high above Rock Creek Park, known as Kalorama, a Greek word meaning beautiful view. At some point in their public lives, Presidents Taft, Harding, Hoover, and Franklin Roosevelt resided in this lovely area.

After a long period of leasing residences for their ambassadors, the French government purchased, in 1936, the four-acre estate of John Hays Hammond, a well-connected millionaire and friend of President Taft. Presumably the French government would have preferred to find a French style chateau for their ambassador's residence, but they settled for this impressive mansion. André de Laboulaye was the first French ambassador to occupy the building, which, at that time, served as both his residence and the embassy offices (chancery). A few years later, the adjoining land lying to the left of the embassy came up for sale and was quickly purchased by the French government to expand the original property, which to some seemed a bit small for such an important residence.

During World War II, when France was controlled by the Vichy government, the United States refused to accept a representative from Vichy, so the residence had no ambassador. However, in late 1944, when Paris was reoccupied, Charles De Gaulle's provisional government sent Henri Bonnet to Washington as ambassador, and he and his wife moved into the mansion. While Bonnet worried about France's huge war debt, his wife Helle undertook to do the official entertaining and she soon became one of Washington's most renowned hostesses.

During the Kennedy administration, Ambassador Herve Alphand and his wife Nicole lived at the residence. Nicole liked to use the semicircular terrace at the back of the residence for entertaining, which sometimes included informal pool parties. When the Alphands left Washington, the stately residence may have lost some of its glamour, but not its importance. De Gaulle stayed there when he attended John Kennedy's funeral and again during his Washington visits in 1981 and 1986. When the President of France, Francois Mitterrand, visited Washington, he too entertained at the mansion.

When the French government opened its new chancery on Reservoir Road in 1968, office space was provided for some 400 staffers. That chancery is said to be France's largest.

The golden brick English Tudor residence with fine gothic detailing is most impressive when viewed from the street. A gated semi-circular driveway leads up to a grand double-door entrance. A huge French flag usually flies above it. An evergreen *Magnolia grandiflora* tree stands at each end of the mansion, and two mature deciduous magnolia trees grace the gates.

To the left of the residence, a long lawn slopes westward from the residence. It is bordered on one side with a wall topped with an iron fence and a hedge of holly bushes that effectively screens the estate from the public street. A special feature of this lawn is the beautifully shaped Norwegian maple that stands alone. Along the right side of the lawn is a fringe of shrubs marking an escarpment that drops off towards Rock Creek Park to the north and is covered with an assortment of trees and shrubs. Next door, to the right of the French residence, is the residence of the Portuguese ambassador.

A walk around to the back of the residence reveals a raised semi-circular marble terrace enclosed with a fine balustrade. Below this terrace the lawn is edged with a beautiful semi-circular bed of blue hydrangeas that repeats the contours of the terrace. Within sight of the terrace is a blue-tinted swimming pool surrounded by azaleas, roses, and bedding plants with a backdrop of dogwood trees. Like many gardens in Washington, this garden comes into its best in April and May.

Between the terrace and the pool, the area is shaded by a very tall Northern Red oak. It is easy to envision this secluded garden filled with guests enjoying champagne and *hors d'oeuvres*. But the beautiful view from the terrace over Rock Creek Park, once a special feature of this property, is now blocked by the growth of mature trees.

This impressive residence has the elegance of a French chateau and is in a lovely setting. The garden in back provides privacy for relaxation, and ample space for large diplomatic functions.

These descending steps from the terrace pass azaleas as they lead to the pool area.

The top of the towering Northern Red oak (*Quercus rubra*) by the terrace can be seen from the front of the residence.

The swimming pool on the edge of the side lawn is surrounded by azaleas, with several dogwoods and rose bushes that provide a good show of color in the spring.

A mature hedge of Bigleaf hydrangea (*Hydrangea macrophylla*) surrounds the rear garden.

Stairs from the marble terrace lead into the semi-circular back lawn.

In these Bigleaf hydrangeas (*Hydrangea macrophylla*), the varying degrees of pH in the whole plant are said to cause variations of color in these mophead flowers.

At the end of October, warm weather in Washington, DC, can cause some azaleas to bloom again as these pink ones have done amidst the still-flowering white vincas and a russet dogwood in full fall color.

The russet fall foliage of a pink dogwood, the green of the bamboo, and the golden hues of hardwoods beyond the pool are part of the vibrant palette of colors surrounding the residence in the fall.

Embassy of the Federal Republic of Germany

The horticultural emphasis here is on landscape design and specimen trees rather than on floral displays.

Six Callery pear trees *(Pyrus calleryana* 'Cleveland Selects') underplanted with begonias, and the grass-like perennial liriope (*Liriope*), shade the entrance to the residence. "Buddy Bear" from Berlin is the greeter standing at the doorway.

61

The Potomac River and Rosslyn, Virginia, can be seen from the terrace of the residence, over the tops of the magnolia trees on the grounds.

The dramatic German residence stands on a plateau at the highest point of a seven-acre estate just west of Georgetown on the site where the old Harriman family villa once stood. Now it is part of a German compound that includes the residence, a large chancery, and several service buildings. The residence is reached by a gated entrance on Foxhall Road, a busy road known for its string of fine homes. A pair of flagstaffs displaying the German and the European Union flags stands just inside the gates.

The entrance driveway makes a loop in front of the residence around an island of six Callery pear tree cultivars known as "Cleveland Select." These trees, opposite the front of the residence, are usually underplanted with bright begonias. A whimsical plastic bear stands at the front door. He is the greeter known as "Buddy Bear" who hails from Berlin, Germany. On a bright day sunglasses are helpful outside the residence, as much light is reflected off the limestone walkways and the walls of the residence.

This stark ambassadorial home was built in 1994 to the design of German architect O.M. Ungers. His idea was to combine the Greek Revival style of Washington's monumental architecture with the modern culture of Germany. The architectural theme of the building is squares, and they are repeated everywhere: window panes are square, the tiles on the terraces and walkways are square; even the little shades on the garden lights are square. This square theme also extends to the square basalt tiles around the pool which in turn are set in square patterns. However, all this hard squareness is in contrast to a soft background of grassy slopes, wooded glens, and curving paths.

The lofty setting of the residence is one of its finest features, as it allows for a long view to the south from the arcade that stretches along the back of the building. The view includes not only the immediate garden and grounds below, but also a distant view over tree tops to the Potomac River. And just to the right, only a mile away, is the glamorous skyline of Rosslyn, Virginia.

Many wisteria vines decorate much of the black iron fence around the property.

Descending from this arcade are two parallel staircases, one at each end of the building. They invite a visit to the shallow reflecting pool below, which is partly screened by 16 magnificent magnolia trees that flank the sides of the stairs. The staircases have landings at the foot of each of three tiers of steps to break the descent and make convenient rest stops when climbing back up. Around the pool area is a broad, tiled apron which becomes the site for occasional large receptions. A rose garden lies at one end of the pool. It is enclosed by a short holly hedge and has trellises for climbers and neat beds planted with other types of roses. A tiny vegetable/cutting garden is found at the side of the residence. The horticultural emphasis here is on landscape design and specimen trees rather than on floral displays.

Bernard Korte, a noted German landscape architect who took on the task of converting a rough and tumble hillside into this park, said "I strove to preserve the existing modulation of the terrain — the ups and downs, [but] I did not want to retain the existing vegetation." That vegetation he described as a dense, impenetrable jungle consisting mostly of acacia and ailanthus trees, many of which were blighted. When clearing the hillside of unbecoming brush and trees, Korte found craters, possibly from Civil War bombardments of Washington. He planted cypress, maples, magnolias, oaks, willows, copper beeches, cherries, ash, dogwoods, and pines on the property, which now have matured and are doing well. The huge lawn is saved from drying out during summer droughts by an extensive underground irrigation system.

The winding asphalt paths were laid down by Korte to follow the natural contours of the land. They provide pleasant walks along the five acres of rolling lawn and tall trees. A half mile of perimeter iron fencing is decorated with about 30 wisteria vines. The walks and glens are delightful, especially when the trees are dressed in their spring or fall colors. The paths are also perfect for diplomatic walks and talks. One path leads to a pleasant duck pond; another to a copse among a stand of holly bushes with wooden benches, a good place for private contemplation or conversations, or perhaps a talk with the elves.

Seriously, these grounds lend themselves well to both contemplation and celebrations. The biggest garden party of the year, German Unity Day, is celebrated by the ambassador on the terraces by his residence with speeches, food, and drink in a "Beer Garden" atmosphere for two to three thousand guests. In sum, this property is not only beautiful and dramatic but seems well suited for both public and private diplomacy.

Potted hibiscus and boxwoods enliven the terrace.

The flagstone terrace along the reflecting pool repeats the square motif.

In the late afternoon, the magnolia trees (*Magnolia grandifolia* 'Little Gem') below the German residence cast deep shadows toward the reflecting pool.

The rose garden by the reflecting pool is enclosed by a short hedge of sheared holly trees.

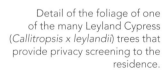

Detail of the foliage of one of the many Leyland Cypress (*Callitropsis x leylandii*) trees that provide privacy screening to the residence.

One of the three sturdy Atlas cedars (*Cedrus atlantica* 'Glauca') located near the reflecting pool.

This pond at the lower end of the garden is cloistered by trees, including weeping willows, oaks, and a Common Bald cypress (*Taxodium distichum*).

A decorative strip of stones curve across the lawn towards a black walnut (*Juglans nigra*) ablaze in its fall colors.

In the fall, a passersby would enjoy the beauty of these maples along the lower edge of the perimeter fence.

This woodland path leads to the pond, then curves up to the terrace.

THE AMBASSADOR'S GARDEN
Apostolic Nunciature of the Holy See

*The cone-shaped fountain splashes
water over lilies in the pond below.*

The Vatican's Embassy in Washington, known as the Apostolic Nunciature of the Holy
See, is the site of the residence garden. Special features of the front are the thirteen
shaped boxwoods along the driveway and two mature pear trees at the corners.

The courtyard at the Nunciature as viewed from the garden.

The Apostolic Nunciature of the Holy See, sometimes referred to as "The Vatican's Embassy," graces the big curve on Massachusetts Avenue known as Observatory Circle. It is directly across the avenue from the U.S. Vice President's home and next door to the Finnish Embassy. The yellow and white flag of the Vatican, emblazoned with the arms of the Holy See, stands above the front door, which is approached by a semi-circular driveway. The face of the embassy is softened by a row of thirteen, well groomed boxwoods.

The noted Catholic architect Frederick V. Murphy designed this three-story Italian Renaissance building for the Holy See in 1939. It first went into use as the office and residence of the Vatican delegation to the United States. It also served as a temporary home for Pope John Paul II while he visited Washington in October 1979. In 1984, during the Reagan presidency, full diplomatic relations were established between the Vatican and the United States. This building, then, was both an embassy and the residence of the ambassador of the Vatican. When Pope Benedict XVI visited Washington in 2008, it served as his temporary home.

The most charming feature of this embassy cannot be seen from the street. It is the small U-shaped cloistered courtyard at the back of the building. In the center of the courtyard is a cone-shaped fountain that splashes water over lilies at its base. This unusual shaped fountain is a one-third scale copy of the bronze Pigna (pine cone) fountain at the Vatican that dates back to the first century. Within the shadowed cloisters of this courtyard, overlooking the fountain, stand the quiescent statues of Pope Pius VI, Saint Peter, and Saint Joseph.

A few steps beyond this courtyard lies a level lawn that spreads out and around a center flower bed ringed by a narrow flagstone walk. The flower bed is like a jewel, well planted with a colorful mix of marigolds, dahlias, begonias, dusty millers, and periwinkles. Around the extremities of the oval-shaped lawn are clusters of yews, hollies, and rhododendrons. A young oak tree near the edge of the lawn was planted in 2008 and ceremoniously blessed by Pope Benedict during his visit to Washington that year. The stand of towering oaks behind the young tree provides welcome shade during hot summers, but allows patches of sunlight to dance over the lawn. When called for, this lawn is a perfect summer setting for party tents, games, and outdoor receptions.

A close look at a far corner of the lawn reveals a gardener's cottage half hidden in the trees. On the adjoining wall facing the garden is a small bas relief plaque of the Madonna and nearby stand two delicate statues of fawns. Unfortunately, real fawns come from the nearby woods by night to feed on the flowers and shrubs of this embassy garden. In another corner of the grounds is a small statute of Saint Francis of Assisi modeled by a former staff member, Monsignor Giovanni Tonucci, who has since been elevated to Archbishop Tonucci. Although his St. Francis keeps an eye on the garden, he doesn't seem at all to intimidate the visiting deer.

This one-third scale copy of the colossal bronze pine cone sculpture "Pigna" at the Vatican, cast in the 1st or 2nd century, is the centerpiece in the courtyard of the Nunciature. In the cloisters of the courtyard are statues of Saint Peter, Saint Joseph, and Pope Pius VI.

Cherry blossoms from a bough of a mature cherry tree.

The courtyard, opens to the wide lawn edged with spring and summer bedding plants and a circular flagstone walkway that invites a serene stroll.

One of two bronze sculptures of deer in the residence garden.

Maples in the garden beginning to change in early fall.

Among hydrangeas and hostas in a corner of the garden is a small sculpture of Saint Francis of Assisi modeled by Archbishop Giovanni Tonucci when he was a staff member at the Nunciature.

The bas relief of Madonna and child in the garden wall above marigolds.

THE AMBASSADOR'S GARDEN
Embassy of Italy

A perfect setting for large and small scale entertaining, de rigueur *in diplomatic life.*

The seal of the Republic of Italy is on the gate to the estate. The driveway to the residence is bordered with colorful azaleas in the spring.

The Italian residence is called "Villa Firenze." It presides over some 22 acres of rolling lawns and thick woodlands bordering Rock Creek Park in Northwest Washington. It is the largest diplomatic spread in the city. The 59-room mansion was designed by architect Russell Kluge and built in 1925 for Blanche Estabrook Roebling O'Brien, a widow. Her late husband was a member of the distinguished Roebling family, builders of the Brooklyn Bridge. The estate was originally named "Estabrook." In the 1930s, Blanche O'Brien leased it to the Hungarian Embassy for several years, but sold it in 1941 to Colonel M. Robert Guggenheim, a World War I veteran, and briefly, Eisenhower's ambassador to Portugal.

Guggenheim and his wife Rebecca, better known as "Polly," had been living aboard his seagoing yacht "Firenze," often anchored on the Potomac River. When the U.S. Navy requested use of the yacht for World War II service, the Guggenheims agreed and sought a new home ashore. When they bought the O'Brien estate, the colonel renamed it "Villa Firenze." Colonel Guggenheim's American-born mother was named Florence which translates into Italian as Firenze. After the colonel died in 1959, Polly remarried and continued to live at Villa Firenze with her second husband, John Logan. They entertained there lavishly, often for charity events. Polly liked to show off her fine collection of glass and John Logan served as chairman of the Cherry Blossom Ball for several years.

The villa became truly Italian only in 1976 when the Italian government purchased it for the residence of the Italian ambassador. Nevertheless, this Tudor-type mansion of stucco and wood timbers with brick and fieldstone additions would fit quite well into the English countryside, except perhaps for its 60-foot swimming pool. The story of the pool is that it was built *before* the house. It seems Blanche O'Brien, the original owner, wanted to observe the construction of the mansion during the summer heat from the cool of the

The Italian and European Union flags fly above the circular drive in front of the residence.

pool. Today only the crest on the iron driveway gates reveals that the property which lies beyond is Italian.

Upon entering through these gates and walking along the shaded driveway, the mansion comes into view, silhouetted against acres of sunlit lawn that sweep away southward and are framed with borders of thick woodland. In the distance there might well be a pair of grazing white-tail deer. Coming upon such a suddenly beautiful view, may require a moment to catch one's breath. It is a truly bucolic scene. The driveway loops around an island of azalea bushes to the front doors of the mansion. Here, on tall flagstaffs, the Italian and European Union flags fly side by side.

As Villa Firenze appears in late summer.

Brilliant orange roses brighten the terrace walls.

Along the back of the house is a broad slate terrace perfect for observing the landscape, dining *al fresco,* or relaxing in the sun. The terrace is host to climbing roses and containers full of colorful plants. A spectacular American elm (*Ulmus americana*) growing beside the sunroom of the house can be seen and enjoyed from many areas of the grounds. The curved driveway disappears downhill as it runs from the residence towards the pool area, one of the few places on the estate level enough to set up banquet tents. The rest of the residence grounds are just too hilly. From the pool area, the villa is barely visible through the trees. One such tree is a statuesque Colorado Blue spruce (*Picea pungens*) that reaches some 80 feet into the sky. A magenta crape myrtle stands alone on a nearby knoll, shining like a beacon in late summer.

On further meandering around the grounds, one passes a young well-shaped cherry tree, a cluster of blue hydrangeas, and a modest greenhouse with a kitchen garden protected from hungry deer by a high fence. The deer problem is probably why a cutting garden is impractical for growing flowers. Two full-time caretakers keep these grounds looking well groomed.

Since the villa has been the Italian ambassador's residence, a long list of distinguished guests have visited the property, including the president of the United States, the president of Italy, prime ministers, supreme court justices, congressional leaders, artists and writers, and eminent representatives of Italian institutions. The Italian ambassadors have made the Villa available for meetings of important cultural, scientific, and humanitarian organizations. It has thus become a special gathering place of cultures and ideas.

The estate, with no neighboring buildings visible, is very private, yet easily accessed from the city and the embassy. The broad terrace overlooking lovely grounds is a perfect setting for large and small scale entertaining, *de rigueur* in the diplomatic life. It also seems an ideal place to collect one's private thoughts, and to enjoy family and close friends in this bucolic setting.

The sweeping view from the terrace of rolling lawn and beyond.

This soaring Colorado blue spruce (*Picea pungens*), that keeps company with a shorter Norway spruce (*Picea abies*) near the pool, appears to be the tallest tree on the estate.

A magnificent American elm (*Ulmus americana*) filters the morning light to make a pattern on the lawn by the sunroom of Villa Firenze.

This spacious terrace, with a long view of the lawn, makes a perfect place for outdoor entertaining.

This large pool, set well away from the residence, has a bath house and marble benches.

A colorful display of spring foliage against the sky at Villa Firenze.

Large snowball viburnum blossoms (*Viburnum opulus*) put on a show at the edge of the lawn.

Ripening cherries on an ornamental dwarf cherry tree (*Prunus* 'Hally Jolivette'), one of the several specimen trees found on the grounds of Villa Firenze.

THE AMBASSADOR'S GARDEN
Embassy of the Republic of Korea

This garden has spaces or "rooms" to surprise and interest the wanderer.

This view of the residence from the semi-circular driveway includes the two crape myrtles that decorate the front of the residence along with flowers in stone pots.

The main terrace of the residence with the "Energy Rock" at its center as seen from the garden.

On a quiet residential street among other fine homes in the Spring Valley section of Northwest Washington is the ambassador's residence of the Republic of Korea. It is embraced by a classic Korean garden, a rarity in the United States, designed for entertaining and relaxation and to remind the ambassador and his wife of their home country.

This multi-level garden was first created in 1986, but had to be dug up when it was discovered the soil of the Spring Valley area contained chemical munitions that the army had tested there during the *First* World War. After the old munitions were removed in 2003, the garden was re-created by the noted Korean-American landscape architect Jeffery Lee. He has said his garden design reflects the landscape of Korea: the high area as North Korea, the brook as the Han River, and the lower area as South Korea where grains are grown, known as the "bread basket of Korea."

Traditional Korean gardens have a special quality. They reflect Korean aesthetics including a desire to live in close harmony with the natural environment. Korean gardens are carefully planned and groomed but are not as formal as Japanese gardens. That is because a Korean garden tends to go with the lay of the land. Pathways meander rather than running straight. Interestingly shaped rocks are featured for their composition and color. Korean gardens also differ from Chinese gardens, which feature rocks and water, in that Koreans usually include a wider range of trees, decorative plants, and flowers. In fact, South Korea even exports flowers, especially chrysanthemums and roses.

From the street level, this garden slopes upward along the northern side of the residence. The garden is reached from the side of the residence by multiple sliding doors that open to a paved terrace. Centered on this terrace is a rough granite rock known as an "Energy Rock." The small paving bricks of this terrace carry the yin and yang as a decorative motif, as also seen on the flag of the Republic of Korea.

The flag of the Republic of Korea adds a touch of color as it flies over the garden.

When Koreans plan their buildings and gardens they pay attention to Feng Shui, an oriental discipline that determines zones of energy and harmony. Another influence in Korean garden design is geomancy, wherein garden alignments are based on points originating from a handful of earth thrown down at random. This is how spiritual qualities are infused into Korean gardens from the start. It is said Korean beliefs about land and nature are quite similar to those traditional to American Indians.

This garden has several interesting decorative features. A Cryptomeria Walk leads from the residence to the upper level of the garden. This walk is along a naturalistic looking path of finely crushed stone and sand, bordered on both sides by tall evergreens underplanted with Solomon's Seal (*Polygonatum commutatum*) of the family Liliaceae. An adjoining path leads to the highest level of the garden, where a classic wooden pavilion stands, said to be fastened together in the traditional manner using only pegs. It is named "Sejong Pavilion" in honor of

This Cryptomeria Walk leads to a stone bench on the upper lawn, useful as a resting place or, when needed, as a serving table by placing a board across the arms.

good King Sejong, who created the Korean alphabet. Such pavilions are typically positioned for viewing the garden and for relaxation and contemplation. Visitors also are invited there for conversation and refreshments, or for a game of mahjongg or chess. This pavilion overlooks the tops of small trees and stands of shrubs. The stone steps that lead up to it are framed with clumps of sedge grass interspersed with a low ground cover that produces tiny purple blossoms at the end of May.

At the northernmost corner of the garden stands a small pagoda made of stone. Only about four feet high, it stands out against a dark leafy background. The low circular wall around it is intended for sitting. Leading up to this pagoda are a series of wide steps. Instead of Korean traditional stone steps, the architect designed these shallow grass steps as a homage to Thomas Jefferson who used low grass steps in his garden.

The brook that originates in the upper garden passes under this bridge and over a small waterfall into a pond of waterlilies.

Waterlilies decorate the two small ponds of the garden.

The Sejong Pavilion, at the highest part of the garden, is named for King Sejong who created the Korean alphabet and was one of Korea's best known kings.

Crossing a shallow brook, these stone steps lead to the upper lawn.

These natural stone steps lead from the driveway up to the garden and past the arbor framing a circular patio used for entertaining.

The arbor at the front of the garden is covered over with the native wisteria (*Wisteria frutescens* 'Amethyst Falls'), a vigorous bloomer.

Meandering further along the curved paths, one comes to a lower level of lawn with a circular stone patio. At its center, the patio has a millstone that once ground corn. Along the back of the patio is a curved trellis decorated with native wisteria (*Wisteria frutescens* "Amethyst Falls"). This patio is a center for outdoor performances and social gatherings, and is used as a serving area for parties. From the patio the ambassador can address his guests and be visible from all levels of the garden.

A path leads from the patio to a small bridge not far away. It spans a brook that cascades over decorative rocks into a small lotus pond below. From the bridge one can see goldfish gliding under the lotus flowers. Reeds gracefully line the banks of the pond and a variety of plants and flowers provides interesting blooms and textures throughout spring, summer, and fall. Beyond the pond and plants is a carpet of moss and green lawn that embraces several decorative gray granite stones. In Korea there is an ancient belief that inanimate objects such as stones and mountains have spirits.

Harmony here is not derived from a single theme or a dominate feature. Instead, the garden has spaces, or "rooms," to surprise and interest the wanderer. Set along the connecting paths are several clean-cut white granite benches with straight sides which are in stark contrast to the naturalism of the garden. They are beautiful in their simplicity, but they hardly look comfortable. However, they have the virtue of being useful as seats and for entertaining. When a board is placed across the two arms they are turned into a convenient table to hold refreshments for garden parties.

Water is an important element in Korean gardens not only for decoration, but for practical purposes such as providing a cooling effect and for plant hydration. Traditionally a pool of water was essential as a standby for fighting fires in the mostly wooden buildings. In this garden, a hidden pump with pipes circulates water though a closed circuit to make the lovely brook. Murky green-colored water is said to be admired in Korean gardens, but in this garden the water is crystal clear.

In early spring this unique garden is full of life with spreads of lilies of the valley and crocuses that are soon followed by pink cherry blossoms. Then in April magnolias and peonies blossom, followed by Solomon's Seal in May, with hydrangeas and irises. In high summer, Black-eyed Susans and Joe Pye Weed flourish, with anemones and beautyberry providing lovely color and textures in late summer. In sum, this seems to be a excellent garden for the private and professional use of His Excellency the Ambassador of the Republic of Korea.

On the edge of the upper lawn boughs of the deciduous Beautyberry shrubs (*Callicarpa dichotoma*) cascade over the large rocks in the area.

Sea oats (*Chasmanthium latifolium*), a perennial ornamental grass, are planted by the brook on the upper lawn as a reminder of the farming traditions of Korea.

Autumn Joy (Stone Crop) sedums (*Sedum telephium* 'Autumn Joy') blossom in the area between the upper and lower lawns and turns a deep russet in late fall.

This path of sand and crushed stone passes alongside crape myrtles and hydrangeas whose dried flower heads have taken on fall color.

A stand of crape myrtles dressed in fall color.

A view from a stand of crape myrtles opposite the circular patio on the lower lawn used for gatherings and entertaining.

Shallow lawn steps, designed with a nod to President Thomas Jefferson's steps at Monticello, lead up to the small stone pagoda.

Royal Netherlands Embassy

More than 3,000 varieties of tulips have been registered according to the Royal Horticultural Association of Holland.

The windows of this Classical Revival residence overlook the front lawn that each spring is planted with masses of tulips and violas.

Princess Irene tulips (*Tulipa* 'Princess Irene') are displayed in ornate black pedestal urns in front of the residence on both sides of the walkway at the edges of the lawn.

O n S Street, just off the Embassy Row stretch of Massachusetts Avenue in one of Northwest Washington's most formal residential areas, is a substantial four-story Classical Revival building.

Over the front doorway flies the red, white, and blue flag of the Netherlands, marking the residence of the Dutch ambassador. Close by are other diplomatic establishments including the residence of the Pakistan ambassador, the residence of the Cyprus ambassador, and the chancery of Chad.

This 30-room mansion was built in 1929 during a time of real estate speculation. It was designed by architect Ward Brown, who drew the plans for Louis Septimus Owsley, a Chicago transportation tycoon. At the time Owsley was president of his own streetcar and elevated line company and an officer in several booming transit companies. In Chicago he was known as the "traction baron." It is not clear how much he used this Washington home, consisting of nine master bedrooms and quarters for seven servants. However, when he retired from business in 1942, he moved to Connecticut and sold the Washington home to the Netherlands government.

The residence has a modest urban garden with little pretense, but in springtime people look for a show of tulips and are seldom disappointed. During the tulip season, the front garden is ablaze with tulips. The bulbs come from Holland by way of a company in Ohio. Early blooming tulips such as Exotic Emperor and Flaming Purissima, which are white and pink, are planted in the preceding fall for blooming in March and early April. For the displays in early May, particularly for European Day, pots of tulips, often orange ones, are placed into the flower beds.

The Netherlands royal family is known formally as The House of Orange-Nassau, so orange tulips are of the royal color. One variety of orange tulips is named after Princess Irene, sister of the present Queen Beatrix. Tulips are also named for celebrities such as the scarlet Bing Crosby tulip, and a red tulip with yellow edges known as the Queen Elizabeth tulip.

Tulips (*Tulipa* in the family *Lilaceae)* were rare in Europe in 1600. The few *Tulipas* imported from Turkey were prized and collected by wealthy landowners. As the bulbs became more available and popular, they were subject to an historic speculative bubble known as "Tulipomania." Prices soared in 1634; then crashed in 1637. At the height of the market, it is said, bulbs were priced at around 3,000 guilders each, about six times the amount of the average person's annual salary at that time.

Tulips thrive in Holland because of the combination of sandy soil and the mild, wet climate. Around 7 million bulbs reportedly are planted in Holland each year. More than 3,000 varieties of tulips have been registered, according to the Royal Horticultural Association of Holland. Tulips are grown commercially in the United States in Skagit Valley, Washington, and in Holland, Michigan.

It is hard to believe any official Dutch garden would be without a good show of tulips. But it has happened. Timing is everything, especially with tulips. During the springtime visit to Washington of Her Majesty Queen Juliana in 1952, it was reported that the imported tulip bulbs were set out in the form of a "J" in the Queen's honor. But due to a dockworkers' strike in New York, the planting was delayed, and the blooms came in too late. Another report alleges that in 1966, when May temperatures hovered around freezing the night before a tulip-time reception, staff members watered the tulips with hot water trying to save the blossoms. When tulips bloom in Washington in April and early May, the blossoms can last for about a week or 10 days unless there are unseasonably hot days, which often occurs in springtime Washington.

Behind the Netherlands ambassador's residence is a small garden consisting of terraces and a lawn enclosed by high walls and bordered with bedding plants, shrubs, and trees. Hollies, nandina, viburnums, crape myrtles, yews, aucubas, and dogwoods all grow there along with trailing hydrangeas, camellias, and late blooming white azaleas. At the center of the lawn stands a small bubbling fountain. Plants in containers provide touches of color on the terraces. A mature *Magnolia grandiflora* tree provides welcome shade in summer. Adjoining the house is a small terrace used for *al fresco* dining.

The Dutch diplomatic establishment in Washington includes a small working greenhouse located on the grounds of the Dutch chancery several miles away. This greenhouse supplies bedding plants for the ambassador's residence and the chancery.

A linguistic note for tulip lovers: "Dutch" refers to the native language and to those who speak it, and "Holland" refers to the coastal part of the Netherlands where tulips are grown.

Princess Irene tulips along the front lawn of the residence.

Cheery Sorbet Hybrid violas are interspersed with the tulips in the front of the residence. This variety is *Viola cornuta* 'Blueberry Cream.'

Early spring tulips Exotic Emperor and Flaming Purissima are underplanted with Sorbet Hybrid violas.

Early spring flowering *Fosteriana* tulips Flaming Purissima and the white Exotic Emperor.

Purple Silver Star grandiflora roses and white Crystalline hybrid tea roses grow in a narrow bed with boxwoods on either side of the entrance to the residence.

The private garden behind the residence includes climbing hydrangeas, crape myrtles, azaleas, acubas, camillas, Oakleaf hydrangeas, viburnums, and dogwood trees. At the far end of this lawn are found yews, hollies, boxwoods, and abelias, with underplanting of hostas and impatiens.

This lower terrace offers another space for entertaining in addition to the garden and upper terrace spaces. Wide sets of stairs connect all three levels.

Far right:
The cherub fountain at the center of the residence garden.

Found! A Morning Dove's nest with one egg in a planter in the residence garden.

This small greenhouse on the embassy grounds is for raising bedding plants for both the residence and chancery.

THE AMBASSADOR'S GARDEN
Royal Norewegian Embassy

"Intimate and informal, yet dignified and friendly"
is an apt description of this pretty garden.

Boxwoods border the front of the residence with topiary arborvitae at
the entry. Displays of pansies compliment the flowering white and pink
dogwoods at the sides of this English Neo-Renaissance style residence.

These trimmed Burford hollies (*Ilex cornuta*), Hicksii yews (*Taxus* x *media* 'Hicksii'), and azaleas are at the side of the residence.

The residence of the Norwegian Ambassador is well situated on Washington's Embassy Row, which the Royal Norwegian Ministry of Foreign Affairs once described as "the most important street in the diplomatic world." The residence occupies the corner of Massachusetts Avenue and 34th Street in Northwest Washington. That puts it right across the street from the well-guarded entrance to the Vice President's home and the Naval Observatory, both of which are screened by trees and nearly invisible from the residence. On the adjoining corner of 34th Street is the serene appearing embassy of the Vatican.

Norway's residence was built in 1931, at the same time that Great Britain was completing its new embassy a short way down Massachusetts Avenue. The designer of the Norwegian residence was John J. Whelan, a well-known American architect, who also designed the South African Embassy nearby on Massachusetts Avenue. Whelan's handsome design for Norway is known as "English Neo-Renaissance," a style popular in the 1930s. At that time the new building was intended to house the Norwegian Legation consisting of only six persons headed by Minister Wilhelm Thorleif von Munthe af Morgenstierne. Upon its completion the minister described his new building to Oslo as being "intimate and informal, yet dignified and friendly."

At President Roosevelt's suggestion in 1942, both the United States and Norway raised their diplomatic missions to embassy level, each headed by an ambassador. Thus, Norway's enlarged mission in Washington required more office space, so a separate chancery was built on the part of the property facing 34th Street. That freed up the original building for conversion into a private residence for the ambassador and provided an area for a garden between the residence and the new chancery.

In front of the residence stands a fine bronze statue of Crown Princess Martha of Norway, who lived in Washington with her young children during much of World War II. The statue, one of the very few in Washington of a

This statue in front of the residence is of Crown Princess Martha who stayed here during World War II.

The garden is centered around this courtyard between the residence (in the background) and the chancery. It is surrounded by perennial borders, with a young Natchez crape myrtle (*Lagerstroemia indica* 'Natchez') at the center.

woman, was created by the Norwegian sculptor Kirsten Kokkin and installed in 2005. Decorating the front of the residence are pink and white dogwoods, with boxwoods in a supporting role. Over the main doorway of the residence flies the swallow-tailed Norwegian flag with its distinctive blue and white Nordic Cross on a red background.

At the left side of the residence, behind a high wall, is a small private terrace of flagstone and grass for the ambassador. It is bordered with plants and shrubs, which gives it an intimate feeling for entertaining visitors. Norwegian birches grace the wall of the residence there and are reminders of Norway's woodlands. Privacy is also provided by a low brick wall that lies between the ambassador's terrace and the larger garden. This wall is backed with blue spruces, crape myrtle, and a large holly tree. Past the spruces is a small side lawn bordered with hollies and azaleas that become a blaze of red, white, and pink colors in April.

The main garden is the courtyard area between the residence and the chancery, carpeted with lawn and bordered with plants and shrubs. A young Natchez crape myrtle grows at the very center of the lawn with under-plantings of colorful tulips and annuals. The garden conveys an intimate feeling that is just right for both entertaining and recreation. This is where Norway's national day on May 17th is usually celebrated. In the perennial borders around the lawn are plantings of shrub roses, iris, peonies, Oakleaf hydrangeas, and purple asters. The rather stark lower windows and walls of the chancery, facing the garden, are softened by evergreens and rose bushes.

Wooden trellises at three of the four corners of this garden are a strong feature. They support mature wisteria vines that produce a fine display of blossoms in May. Outside on the garden wall along 34th Street is a fretwork of well-espaliered pyracantha that makes a bright show of orange berries in September.

Perhaps the most surprising feature in this modest garden is the lap pool. It lies just inside the privacy wall along 34th Street. One end of the pool faces the residence, the other end faces the chancery. The pool is 60 feet long and six feet wide. It is covered by a roof and open to the garden, but is somewhat screened by plantings. At first sight, this type of pool might seem like a folly, but Norwegian diplomats say it is very useful for keeping in shape during summers, and a few of the more hearty Norwegians claim it is useful even in winter.

The description some 80 years ago of the residence as being "intimate and informal, yet dignified and friendly," is also a very fitting description of this diplomatic garden today.

The show of wisteria on the trellises in April.

This walkway, by a Japanese maple and an American holly, leads down to the garden from the side terrace of the residence.

Russet Oakleaf hydrangeas and asters provide this colorful fall display beside the pool.

Alpine poppies (*Papaver alpinum*) grow in a garden pot with other annuals.

A view of the courtyard from a walkway by the pool, seen from under the trellis that supports the wisteria.

Climbing roses share the trellis below the vines of the wisteria.

Birch trees in fall coloration line one side of the ambassador's private terrace. Also bordering this terrace are three Norway spruces.

The lap pool at the edge of the garden offers close-up views of the flowers in the perennial border along its side.

THE AMBASSADOR'S GARDEN
Embassy of Sweden

The view from the terrace includes a sweeping lawn that gently slopes away from the residence to the distant tennis court.

Under the yellow and blue Swedish flag on the front lawn of the Swedish residence are a red maple, a gingko, and several crape myrtle trees.

The carved stonework around the front door includes the three crowns of the Swedish coat of arms. On the terrace are large hibiscus plants.

The architecture of the Swedish residence may be a bit of a surprise because it does not resemble anything Swedish. It is a Californian Mission-style building, a type of architecture very fashionable in Washington in the 1920s.

Nevertheless, it is an attractive mansion set well back from busy Nebraska Avenue that runs along a ridge on one of the higher elevations of Northwest Washington. American University is a near neighbor and next door over the garden wall is the residence of the Japanese ambassador. The Swedish residence was built in 1922 to the design of Arthur B. Heaton, a noted Washington architect. It is a hacienda-type mansion built for David Lawrence, founder of the magazine *US News & World Report*. Years later, in 1959, the Swedish government purchased the building from Lawrence to be the residence for the ambassador.

The estate is fronted by a semi-circular driveway that sweeps in from the entrance gate to the front door and on around to an exit gate, thus enclosing a wide expanse of lawn. The colors of Sweden fly from a tall flagstaff on the lawn, affirming that the territory is indeed Swedish rather than Californian. That point is further made by the Royal Swedish emblem carved in stone over the doorway. The front lawn is host to several crape myrtles, a gingko, and a red maple. Framing the front doorway during warm weather are a pair of red hibiscus plants that winter over in a sunroom. In summer, bursts of red shrub roses decorate the front terrace along with boxwoods and plantings of annuals.

The site for Swedish garden parties and receptions is just to the left of the residence on a level lawn bordered with oaks, underplanted with rounded boxwoods, azaleas, lilacs (which are very popular in Sweden), and peonies. This also is the place for the celebration of Sweden's National Day on June 6th. Sweden's membership in the European Union is symbolized by the blue flag with a circle of gold stars displayed on this lawn from a special flagstaff.

A flagstone terrace and lawn run along the back of the residence. Here, in the shade of an awning, wicker furniture and a coffee table provide for *al fresco* reading,

Peonies (*Paeonia*) thrive with the additional light reflected off the white walls on the left side of the residence.

A low branch of this oak tree supports a romantic wooden swing. From it the whole lawn at the back of the residence can be viewed.

refreshments, and conversation. On the wall here is a small green-bronze sculpture by Sweden's Carl Milles that oversees this private oasis.

The view from the terrace includes a sweep of lawn that gently slopes away from the residence toward the ambassador's distant tennis court – far enough away so the noise of the game does not disturb the quiet of the residence. The court has hosted such Swedish tennis greats as Björn Borg, Stefan Edberg, and Mats Wilander. When the senior George Bush was vice president, he too played here with the ambassador.

Much nearer to the residence, an inviting swing hangs from a strong limb of an oak tree. It is a perfect perch from which to enjoy the long view toward the tennis court. That view looks much like a pastoral scene – minus the grazing sheep. Several attractive specimen trees grace the lawn, including an American sweet gum. Newly planted apple saplings will produce Swedish apples known as Rambos. The saplings' ancestors were brought to America in 1639, in the form of seeds, by Swedish immigrants from the town of Ramberga, hence the name Rambo. They have since become a popular variety now found in Pennsylvania and Virginia.

Also from the swing, a small summer greenhouse can be seen across the lawn. White roses grow alongside it. The kitchen garden nearby is encircled by a high fence necessary to exclude deer, the abiding nuisance to gardeners even in this well populated residential neighborhood. Grown in this garden, to the chef's requirements, are fancy lettuces, tomatoes, chives, mint, and an assortment of herbs.

As a transition between the intimate terrace and lower level back lawn, a shallow bank of perennials lies between them, cut through by a path and several steps. On each side of the steps, the bank is planted with a mix of hydrangeas, daylilies, lavenders, a butterfly bush, salvia, iris, and roses. Also during spring and summer, annuals in containers are placed around the terrace to provide splashes of color. Blue and yellow pansies are often in the front entry way, as they show the national colors of Sweden.

Roses and salvia in the perennial border above the lower lawn.

Like many grand residences and fine homes, the Swedish ambassador's residence has a high demand for cut flowers and greenery for flower arrangements. In early spring branches of forsythia are brought in from the garden for large floral arrangements. The same is done when the cherry trees are in bloom. Dahlias and peonies grown on the grounds also provide armloads of flowers for special displays. To extend the life of these cut flowers the residence has a walk-in cooler for preserving the blossoms when they are not out on display.

Even if the residence itself doesn't look very Swedish, the garden does, with earmarks of a typically charming Swedish garden, namely a well-kept lawn, lovely trees, including apple trees, and, of course, lilac bushes.

Roses and salvia along the edge of the upper lawn.

This small bronze sculpture by Carl Milles, Sweden's most renowned sculptor, overlooks the stone terrace.

Lavender in the foreground grows with Russian sage (*Perovskia*) and other perennials along the top of the lower lawn.

Peonies (*Paeonia*) thrive by a low stone wall along the terrace lawn. The vigorous Boston ivy (*Parthenocissus tricuspidata*) that adorns a wing of the residence turns scarlet in the fall, but is scheduled for removal.

The lawn along the left side of the residence is bordered by a variety of trees and edged by hostas. Peonies and lilies grow in the bed under the arched windows.

The tennis court in the lower lawn area is partly sheltered by deciduous hardwood trees.

This charming little greenhouse on the back lawn is embraced by small evergreens and roses.

A back view of this California-mission style residence.

BIBLIOGRAPHY

BOOKS

Bonar, Ann. *Tulips,* Pavilion Books Limited, 1993.

Brickell, Christopher, Henry Marc Cathey and H. Marc Cathey. *American Horticultural Society A to Z Encyclopedia of Garden Plants*, DK Publishing, 2004.

Brown, Jane. *Garden of a Golden Afternoon:* The Story of a Partnership: Edward Lutyens and Gertrude Jekyll, New York: Van Nostrand Reinhold Co., 1982.

Browne, Janet. *Roses,* Pavilion Books Limited, 1993.

Cathey, Dr. H. Marc. *Heat-Zone Gardening,* Time Life Books, 1998, ©1998 American Horticultural Society.

Coombes, Allen J. *Dictionary of Plant Names,* Timber Press, 1993.

Dirr, Michael A. *Manual of Woody Landscape Plants, 4th Edition.* Stipes Publishing, 1975.

FitzGerald, Olda. *Irish Gardens,* Hearst Books, 1999. From the Editors of Country Living Gardener.

Griswold, Mac and Eleanor Weller. *The Golden Age of American Gardens,* Harry Abrams, Inc. in Association with The Garden Club of America, 1991.

Harlow, William M. and Ellwood S. Harrar. *Textbook of Dendrology,* McGraw-Hill Book Company, Inc. New York and London,1937.

Highsmith, Carol M. and Ted Landphair. *Embassies in Washington,* The Preservation Press, National Trust for Historic Preservation,1992.

Jenssen, Hugo Lauritz and Guri Dahl. Representativt: *Buildings in the Foreign Service,* Forlaget Press, 2008. (Norway)

Nicholson, B.E. *The Illustrated Book of Garden Flowers,* Peerage Books, London, revised 1979.

Stacy, L. *Great American Gardens,* New Line Books, 2006.

Tishler, William H. Editor. *American Landscape Architecture,* The Preservation Press, 1989.

Wells, Diana. *100 Flowers: and How They Got Their Names,* Algonquin Books of Chapel Hill,1997.

ARTICLES

Higgins, Adrian. "Reimagining the Traditional English Garden," *The Washington Post*, May 7, 2009.

_____. "Going Green, Diplomatically," *The Washington Post*, December 15, 2011.

Turek, Leslie. *Garden Rooms in the Arts and Crafts Garden,* for the Radcliffe Seminars course "The Arts and Craft Garden," 10 November 1993.

Van Dyne, Larry. "DC's Best Embassies," *Washingtonian Magazine*, February, 2008.

Dan, Sharon Jaffe. "Private Tour-Villa Firenze," *Home and Design Magazine,* May/June 2010.

BROCHURES

"The British Ambassador's Residence Washington, DC," published by, the Government Art Collection of the United Kingdom, 2004.

Korte, Berhard, Dr. "The Park at the German Ambassador's Residence in Washington, DC," published by the German Embassy, Washington DC, 2006.

"Korea People & Culture," published by Korean Culture and Information Service, January 2011.